HOW TO START, INVEST AND EARN WITH CRYTPO CURRENCY

A BEGINNER'S GUIDE ON CRYTPO CURRENCY

ALABI GODSPEED

Copyright © 2024 ALABI GODSPEED

All rights reserved

The characters and events portrayed in this book are fictitious. Any similarity to real persons, living or dead, is coincidental and not intended by the author.

No part of this book may be reproduced, or stored in a retrieval system, or transmitted in any form or by any means, electronic, mechanical, photocopying, recording, or otherwise, without express written permission of the publisher.

ISBN:9798325271809

Cover design by: Art Painter
Library of Congress Control Number: 2018675309
Printed in the United States of America

To all the pioneers and adventurers venturing into the captivating realm of cryptocurrency,

This dedication is for you - the bold, the curious, the seekers of knowledge and opportunity. Whether you're taking your first steps or have already embarked on the exhilarating journey of cryptocurrency, this book is dedicated to your courage, your curiosity, and your determination to chart new territories in the ever-evolving landscape of finance.

For the beginners, eager to unlock the mysteries of blockchain and digital assets, may this guide be your compass, guiding you through the uncharted waters with clarity and confidence. Your willingness to explore, learn, and grow inspires us all.

For the seasoned users, navigating the highs and lows of the crypto market with resilience and wisdom, may this book offer fresh insights, new strategies, and a renewed sense of purpose on your ongoing journey. Your experience and expertise enrich the community and pave the way for others to follow.

Together, let us embrace the transformative power of cryptocurrency - to start anew, to invest wisely, and to earn with purpose. May this dedication serve as a testament to our shared commitment to innovation, empowerment, and financial freedom for all.

With boundless gratitude and optimism,

Alabi Godspeed

CONTENTS

Title Page
Copyright
Dedication
Introduction
Preface

CHAPTER 1	1
CHAPTER 2	4
CHAPTER 3	8
CHAPTER 4	12
CHAPTER 5	17
Acknowledgement	19
About The Author	21

INTRODUCTION

Welcome to "The Beginner's Guide to Cryptocurrency: A Comprehensive Handbook on Starting, Investing, and Earning." In recent years, cryptocurrency has emerged as a transformative force in the world of finance, offering individuals unprecedented opportunities for investment, financial freedom, and innovation. This book is designed to provide beginners with a comprehensive overview of cryptocurrency, from its basic principles to advanced investment strategies and earning opportunities. Whether you're a newcomer curious about the world of digital assets or an experienced investor looking to expand your knowledge, this guide will equip you with the essential tools and insights needed to navigate the dynamic and rapidly evolving landscape of cryptocurrency. Through clear explanations, real-world examples,

and practical tips, we aim to demystify cryptocurrency and empower you to make informed decisions in your journey towards financial independence. Let's embark on this exciting adventure together and unlock the full potential of cryptocurrency!

PREFACE

As the author of "The Beginner's Guide to Cryptocurrency," I am thrilled to present this comprehensive handbook to readers who are eager to explore the world of digital assets. My journey into the world of cryptocurrency began with curiosity and a desire to understand the underlying technology and its potential impact on the future of finance. Along the way, I encountered challenges, made mistakes, and learned valuable lessons that I am excited to share with you in this book. My goal is to provide readers with a clear and accessible resource that empowers them to navigate the complexities of cryptocurrency with confidence and clarity. I hope that this book serves as a valuable tool for beginners embarking on their cryptocurrency journey and inspires curiosity, exploration, and growth in the ever-changing world of digital assets.

CHAPTER 1

INTRODUCTION TO CRYPTOCURRENCY

Cryptocurrency has rapidly transformed the financial landscape, offering individuals unprecedented opportunities for financial freedom and investment. In this chapter, we'll delve into the fundamentals of cryptocurrency, exploring its origins, key concepts, and how it has revolutionized the way we perceive and interact with money.

Understanding the Basics

Cryptocurrency, at its core, is a digital or virtual form of currency that operates independently of traditional banking systems and central authorities. Unlike fiat currency, which is controlled by governments and central

banks, cryptocurrencies are decentralized and rely on cryptographic techniques for secure transactions.

The most famous example of cryptocurrency is Bitcoin, introduced in 2009 by the mysterious Satoshi Nakamoto. Bitcoin paved the way for thousands of other cryptocurrencies, each with its unique features, use cases, and value propositions.

The Evolution of Cryptocurrency

Since the inception of Bitcoin, the cryptocurrency ecosystem has evolved significantly, with new technologies and innovations continuously reshaping the landscape. Cryptocurrencies like Ethereum, Ripple, and Litecoin have emerged, each offering distinct advantages and use cases. One of the most groundbreaking developments in cryptocurrency is blockchain technology. A blockchain is a decentralized ledger that records all transactions across a network of computers, ensuring transparency, security, and immutability. This technology forms the foundation of most cryptocurrencies and has applications beyond

finance, including supply chain management, voting systems, and decentralized applications (DApps).

Key Concepts: Blockchain Technology, Wallets, and Exchanges

Understanding key concepts is essential for navigating the world of cryptocurrency effectively. Here are some fundamental concepts every beginner should know:

Blockchain Technology: As mentioned earlier, blockchain technology is the underlying technology behind most cryptocurrencies. It consists of a chain of blocks, each containing a record of transactions, linked together in a chronological order. This decentralized and transparent ledger ensures the integrity and security of transactions.

Wallets: Cryptocurrency wallets are digital tools used to store, send, and receive cryptocurrencies. There are various types of wallets, including hardware wallets (e.g.,

Ledger Nano S), software wallets (e.g., Exodus), and online wallets (e.g., Coinbase Wallet). Each wallet comes with its unique features and security considerations.

Exchanges: Cryptocurrency exchanges are online platforms where users can buy, sell, and trade cryptocurrencies. Some popular exchanges include Coinbase, Binance, and Kraken. These platforms provide liquidity and facilitate price discovery in the cryptocurrency market.

Now that we've covered the basics of cryptocurrency, let's move on to the next chapter, where we'll explore the steps to getting started with cryptocurrency.

CHAPTER 2

GETTING STARTED WITH CRYPTOCURRENCY

Entering the world of cryptocurrency can be both exciting and intimidating for beginners. In this chapter, we'll guide you through the essential steps to start your journey into the world of cryptocurrency.

Step 1: Education and Research

Before diving into cryptocurrency investing, it's crucial to educate yourself about the market, technology, and risks involved. There are numerous resources available, including online courses, books, and reputable websites, that can provide valuable insights into the crypto space. Additionally, joining online communities and forums can help you stay updated on the latest trends and developments.

For example, platforms like Coursera and Udemy offer comprehensive courses on cryptocurrency and blockchain technology, covering topics such as Bitcoin basics, Ethereum smart contracts, and decentralized finance (DeFi). Reading books like "Mastering Bitcoin" by Andreas M. Antonopoulos and "The Bitcoin Standard" by Saifedean Ammous can also deepen your understanding of cryptocurrency.

Step 2: Choosing a Reliable Exchange

Once you've gained a basic understanding of cryptocurrency, the next step is to choose a reliable exchange where you can buy, sell, and trade cryptocurrencies. When selecting an exchange, consider factors such as security, fees, supported cryptocurrencies, and user interface. Some of the most popular cryptocurrency exchanges include Coinbase, Binance, and Kraken. Coinbase is known for its user-friendly interface and strong security measures, making it an excellent choice for beginners. Binance offers a wide range of cryptocurrencies and advanced trading features, catering to both novice and experienced traders. Kraken is renowned for its robust security measures and high liquidity, making it a preferred choice for institutional investors.

Step 3: Creating Your Wallet

After choosing an exchange, you'll need to create a cryptocurrency wallet to store your digital assets securely. Wallets come in various forms, including hardware wallets, software wallets, and online wallets. Hardware wallets, such as Ledger Nano S and Trezor, are physical devices that store your private keys offline, offering maximum security. Software wallets, like Exodus and Atomic Wallet, are applications that run on your computer or smartphone, providing convenience and accessibility. Online wallets, such as Coinbase Wallet and MyEtherWallet, are web-based platforms that allow you to access your funds from any device with an internet connection.

When creating a wallet, remember to keep your private keys safe and never share them with anyone. Losing your private keys can result in the loss of your cryptocurrency holdings, so it's essential to back them up securely.

Step 4: Identity Verification

Most reputable cryptocurrency exchanges require users to verify their identity before trading. This process, known as Know Your Customer (KYC) verification, helps exchanges comply with regulatory requirements and prevent fraudulent activities, such as money laundering and terrorism financing. To verify your identity, you'll typically need to provide personal information, such as your full name, date of birth, address, and government-issued ID. Some exchanges may also require additional documents, such as proof of address and source of funds.

Step 5: Making Your First Purchase

Once your account is verified, you can fund it with fiat currency (e.g., USD, EUR) and start buying cryptocurrencies. Most exchanges offer multiple payment methods, such as bank transfers, credit/debit cards, and cryptocurrency deposits. Choose the payment method that best suits your preferences and proceed with the transaction.

When buying cryptocurrencies, it's essential to start with small investments and diversify your portfolio to mitigate risk. Cryptocurrency markets can be highly volatile, and prices can fluctuate dramatically within a short period, so it's crucial to invest responsibly.

CHAPTER 3

INVESTING IN CRYPTOCURRENCY

Now that you've set up your account and made your first purchase, it's time to explore the world of cryptocurrency investing. In this chapter, we'll discuss essential tips and strategies for investing wisely in cryptocurrency.

Conducting Research: The Foundation of Successful Investing

Before investing in any cryptocurrency, it's essential to conduct thorough research to understand its technology, use case, team, and market potential. Many cryptocurrencies claim to offer innovative solutions to real-world problems, but not all of them deliver on their promises. By delving into the fundamentals of a project, you can make informed decisions and avoid falling victim to scams and fraudulent schemes.

For example, let's consider Ethereum, the second-largest cryptocurrency by market capitalization. Ethereum is a decentralized platform that enables developers to build and deploy smart contracts and decentralized applications (DApps). Its native cryptocurrency, Ether (ETH), is used to pay for transactions and computational services on the Ethereum network. By understanding Ethereum's underlying technology and ecosystem, investors can assess its long-term potential and make informed investment decisions.

Diversification: Spreading Your Risks

Diversification is a fundamental principle of investing that involves spreading your investments across different assets to minimize risk. In the world of cryptocurrency, diversification can help you mitigate the volatility and uncertainty inherent in the market.

There are several ways to diversify your cryptocurrency portfolio, including investing in multiple cryptocurrencies, allocating funds across different sectors or industries, and incorporating traditional assets like stocks and bonds. By diversifying your portfolio, you can reduce the impact of adverse events and increase your chances of achieving long-term financial success.

For example, let's say you have $10,000 to invest in cryptocurrency. Instead of putting all your money into a single cryptocurrency like Bitcoin, you could allocate a portion of your funds to other top-performing cryptocurrencies like Ethereum, Binance Coin, and Cardano. By diversifying your portfolio, you can spread your risks and capture opportunities across multiple assets.

Staying Informed: Keeping Up with Market Trends

In the fast-paced world of cryptocurrency, staying informed is essential for making timely investment decisions and capitalizing on emerging trends. There are various sources of information available, including cryptocurrency news websites, social media platforms, and online forums.

For example, platforms like CoinDesk, CoinTelegraph, and CryptoSlate provide up-to-date news, analysis, and insights into the cryptocurrency market. Following influential figures and thought leaders in the crypto space on social media platforms like Twitter and LinkedIn can also help you stay updated on the latest developments and market trends.

Risk Management: Protecting Your Investments

Risk management is a critical aspect of successful investing that involves identifying, assessing, and mitigating risks to protect your investments. In the world of cryptocurrency, where volatility and uncertainty are prevalent, effective risk management strategies are essential for preserving capital and achieving long-term financial goals.

There are several risk management techniques you can employ when investing in cryptocurrency, including setting clear investment goals, establishing stop-loss orders, and diversifying your portfolio. By defining your risk tolerance and implementing appropriate risk management measures, you can navigate the crypto market with confidence and peace of mind.

For example, let's say you decide to invest $1,000 in Bitcoin. To manage your risk effectively, you could set a stop-loss order at 10% below the current market price. If the price of Bitcoin falls below this threshold, the exchange will automatically sell your position, limiting your losses and preserving capital.

CHAPTER 4

EARNING WITH CRYPTOCURRENCY

In addition to traditional investing, there are several ways to earn passive income with cryptocurrency. In this chapter, we'll explore some popular methods for generating income and maximizing returns in the world of cryptocurrency.

Staking: Participating in Proof-of-Stake Networks

Staking is a process that involves actively participating in the validation and consensus mechanisms of a blockchain network. Unlike traditional mining, which relies on computational power to secure the network, staking relies on the ownership of cryptocurrency tokens to validate transactions and produce new blocks. Proof-of-stake (PoS) is a consensus mechanism used by many cryptocurrencies, including Ethereum 2.0, Cardano, and Tezos. In a PoS network, validators are chosen to create new blocks and validate transactions based on the number of tokens they hold and are willing to "stake" as collateral.

By staking your cryptocurrency tokens, you can earn rewards in the form of additional tokens or transaction fees. The more tokens you stake, the higher your chances of being selected as a validator and earning rewards. Staking provides a passive income stream for cryptocurrency holders while contributing to the security and decentralization of the network.

For example, let's consider Tezos (XTZ), a blockchain platform that uses a PoS consensus mechanism. Tezos holders can delegate their tokens to a validator, known as a "baker," to participate in the staking process and earn rewards. Bakers are responsible for creating new blocks and validating transactions on the Tezos network, and they receive a portion of the rewards generated from staking.

Mining: Harnessing Computational Power for Rewards

Mining is the process of using computational power to validate and process transactions on a blockchain network. Miners compete to solve complex mathematical puzzles and add new blocks to the blockchain, and they are rewarded with newly minted cryptocurrency tokens for their efforts.

Bitcoin mining is perhaps the most well-known example of cryptocurrency mining, where miners use specialized hardware called ASICs (Application-Specific Integrated Circuits) to perform complex calculations and secure the Bitcoin network. However, mining is not limited to Bitcoin, and many other cryptocurrencies, such as Ethereum and Litecoin, can be mined using different algorithms and hardware configurations.

Mining can be a profitable venture for those with access to cheap electricity and specialized mining hardware. However, it requires a significant upfront investment in equipment and infrastructure, as well as ongoing maintenance and operational costs. Additionally, the mining landscape is highly competitive, with diminishing returns over time as more miners join the network.

For example, let's say you decide to start mining Ethereum using a GPU (Graphics Processing Unit) mining rig. You would need to purchase the necessary hardware, such as graphics cards, power supplies, and cooling systems, and set up a dedicated mining rig to begin mining Ethereum. As a miner, you would earn rewards in the form of Ether (ETH) for validating transactions and securing the Ethereum network.

Yield Farming: Maximizing Returns through DeFi Protocols

Yield farming, also known as liquidity mining, is a strategy that involves providing liquidity to decentralized finance (DeFi) protocols in exchange for rewards. DeFi refers to a set of financial services and applications built on blockchain technology, such as lending, borrowing, and trading, that operate without intermediaries like banks or financial institutions.

Yield farming allows users to earn interest, trading fees, or governance tokens by participating in liquidity pools or lending platforms. Liquidity providers deposit their cryptocurrency tokens into smart contracts, where they are used to facilitate trading and other activities on the platform. In return, liquidity providers receive rewards in the form of additional tokens or a share of the platform's fees.

For example, let's consider Uniswap, a decentralized exchange (DEX) that allows users to swap ERC-20 tokens directly from their wallets. Uniswap operates using automated market maker (AMM) algorithms, which rely on liquidity pools to facilitate trading. Users can earn rewards by providing liquidity to Uniswap's liquidity pools, known as "liquidity providers" or "LPs," in exchange for a share of the trading fees generated on the platform.

Masternodes: Supporting Networks for Passive Income

Masternodes are full nodes in a cryptocurrency network that perform specific functions, such as facilitating transactions, providing privacy features, or supporting network governance. Unlike regular nodes, which passively relay transactions and maintain a copy of the blockchain, masternodes perform additional tasks and are rewarded for their contributions to the network.

Masternodes typically require users to stake a certain amount of cryptocurrency as collateral to qualify for participation. In return, masternode operators receive rewards in the form of additional cryptocurrency tokens for their efforts. Masternodes provide a passive income stream for cryptocurrency holders while supporting the security and functionality of the network.

For example, let's consider Dash, a cryptocurrency that uses a two-tier network consisting of regular nodes and masternodes. Masternodes perform specialized functions, such as InstantSend and PrivateSend, and receive rewards in the form of Dash tokens for their services. To operate a masternode, users must stake a minimum of 1,000 Dash as collateral, which serves as an incentive to support the network and maintain its integrity.

CHAPTER 5

CONCLUSION AND NEXT STEPS

Congratulations! You've made it to the end of this comprehensive guide to cryptocurrency. By now, you should have a solid understanding of the basics of cryptocurrency, how to get started, essential tips for investing wisely, and various methods for earning passive income.

As you embark on your cryptocurrency journey, remember that education, research, and ongoing learning are key to success in this dynamic and rapidly evolving space. Keep exploring new projects, staying informed about market trends, and refining your investment strategies to maximize your potential returns and achieve your financial goals.

Whether you're a seasoned investor or a beginner exploring the world of cryptocurrency for the first time, there's

never been a better time to get involved. With the right knowledge, tools, and mindset, you can unlock the full potential of cryptocurrency and embark on a rewarding financial journey.

I hope you find this eBook comprehensive and informative. Let me know if there are any additional details you'd like to include or if you have any other questions!

ACKNOWLEDGEMENT

I would like to express my sincere gratitude to everyone who contributed to the creation of this book. To my family and friends, thank you for your unwavering support and encouragement throughout this journey. Your belief in me has been a constant source of inspiration and motivation. I am also deeply grateful to the team at [Publisher Name], whose expertise and dedication brought this project to life. Special thanks to [Editor Name] for their insightful feedback and guidance, and to [Designer Name] for their creative vision and design expertise. Additionally, I would like to acknowledge the countless individuals, educators, and thought leaders in the cryptocurrency community who generously share their knowledge and insights, shaping the future of this exciting industry. Finally, to the readers of this book, thank you for embarking on this journey with me. I hope that the information and insights presented in these pages

empower you to navigate the world of cryptocurrency with confidence and clarity.

ABOUT THE AUTHOR

Alabi Godspeed

Alabi Godspeed is a seasoned financial expert and passionate advocate for emerging technologies. With a deep-rooted interest in cryptocurrency and blockchain, Alabi has dedicated years to exploring the intricacies of digital assets and decentralized finance.

Drawing from extensive experience in investment management and financial planning, Alabi brings a wealth of knowledge and expertise to the world of cryptocurrency. Through meticulous research and hands-on experience, he has developed a keen understanding of cryptocurrency investing strategies and market dynamics.

As a firm believer in financial education and empowerment, Alabi is committed to sharing his insights and expertise with others. Through writing, speaking engagements, and educational initiatives, he strives to demystify cryptocurrency and help individuals achieve their financial goals.

With a focus on practicality and accessibility, Alabi is dedicated to helping readers navigate the complexities of the cryptocurrency market and seize new opportunities for financial growth and prosperity.

www.ingramcontent.com/pod-product-compliance
Lightning Source LLC
Chambersburg PA
CBHW031600210526
45464CB00003B/1360